STUDY GUIDE

HOW

LEADERS

CREATE

CHAOS

STUDY GUIDE

HOW

LEADERS

CREATE

CHAOS

AND WHY THEY SHOULD!

SAM CHAND

AVAIL

CONTENTS

CHAPTER 1

STABILITY ISN'T YOUR FRIEND!

"Every innovative idea creates chaos."

REFLECT AND TAKE ACTION:

In your own words, what are the pros
and cons of stability?

_____

_____

_____

_____

_____

_____

Think back to a time of stability in
your organization. What was going
well? What was going awry?

_____

_____

_____

_____

_____

_____

What do you think precedes all periods
of instability and chaos?

_____

_____

_____

_____

_____

_____

> *Aware of their discussion, Jesus asked them: "Why are you talking about having no bread? Do you still not see or understand? Are your hearts hardened? Do you have eyes but fail to see, and ears but fail to hear? And don't you remember?"*
>
> *Mark 8:17-18*

Consider the scripture above and answer the following questions:

What does the above passage reveal about communicating vision?

_____

_____

_____

_____

_____

_____

Do you think you'll ever face pushback when you present a big vision, as Jesus did in this passage?

_____

_____

_____

_____

_____

_____

Why do you think the disciples were concerned with not having enough bread?

_____

_____

_____

_____

_____

_____

What are some reasons that leaders become timid and complacent regarding their vision?

_____

_____

_____

_____

_____

_____

Has unexpected chaos ever helped you grow in a relationship? Describe the experience.

_____

_____

_____

_____

_____

_____

_____

Are you willing to bring about chaos to implement a big idea? Do you think it's worth it? Why?

_____

_____

_____

_____

_____

_____

_____

How will being more intentional in meetings change your organization?

_____

_____

_____

_____

_____

_____

_____

NOT A NEW IDEA

"The coming of Jesus' kingdom doesn't resolve all the chaos now. Someday, in the new heavens and new earth, every wrong will be made right, but until then, we live in the tension between 'the already' and 'the not yet.'"

READING TIME

As you read
Chapter 2:
"Not a New
Idea" in
*How Leaders
Create Chaos*,
reflect on the
questions and
scriptures.

REFLECT AND TAKE ACTION:

How do you lead your team when
faced with chaos? Does your leadership style change?

_____

_____

_____

_____

_____

_____

What are some biblical or historical
instances of Christian men and women
stepping up amidst chaos?

_____

_____

_____

_____

_____

_____

What about Martin Luther's story
jumps out to you? Were you previously
unaware of any aspect of his journey?

_____

_____

_____

_____

_____

_____

> But when he saw many of the Pharisees and Sadducees coming to where he was baptizing, he said to them: "You brood of vipers! Who warned you to flee from the coming wrath? Produce fruit in keeping with repentance. And do not think you can say to yourselves, 'We have Abraham as our father.' I tell you that out of these stones God can raise up children for Abraham. The ax is already at the root of the trees, and every tree that does not produce good fruit will be cut down and thrown into the fire.
>
> Matthew 3:7-10

Consider the scripture above and answer the following questions:

What "fruit" do you think John the Baptist is referring to in this passage?

_____

_____

_____

_____

_____

_____

Do you think what John says in this passage caused chaos and disruption among the Pharisees and Sadducees? Why or why not?

_____

_____

_____

_____

_____

_____

In the early days of the church, how did the apostles create chaos? Was this chaos necessary?

_____

_____

_____

_____

_____

_____

Have you ever trusted God in the midst of chaos? What was the result?

_____

_____

_____

_____

_____

_____

Have you ever been motivated by someone else's response to chaos? What did they do that inspired you?

_____

_____

_____

_____

_____

_____

_____

When people think of your leadership, do you think they see a house cat or a lion? What's the difference?

_____

_____

_____

_____

_____

_____

_____

_____

CHAPTER 3

PLANNED CHAOS OR SURPRISED DISRUPTION?

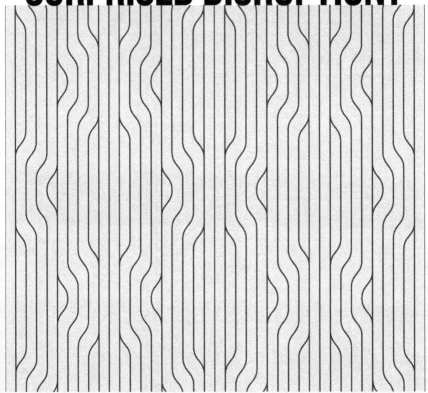

*"Sometimes, an unexpected opportunity
is the cause of chaos."*

READING TIME

As you read Chapter 3: "Planned Chaos or Surprised Disruption?" in *How Leaders Create Chaos*, reflect on the questions and scriptures.

REFLECT AND TAKE ACTION:

Has an opportunity within your organization ever led to unexpected chaos? Describe the experience.

_____
_____
_____
_____
_____
_____

If you knew that an amazing opportunity was tied to chaos, would you still take it? Explain your answer.

_____
_____
_____
_____
_____
_____

What do you think are the main differences between managers and leaders?

_____
_____
_____
_____
_____
_____

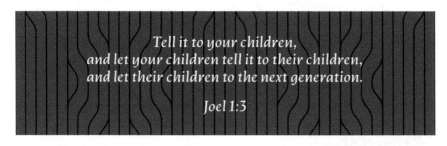

> Tell it to your children,
> and let your children tell it to their children,
> and let their children to the next generation.
>
> Joel 1:3

Consider the scripture above and answer the following questions:

What does the above verse reveal about storytelling?

_____

_____

_____

_____

_____

_____

Do you share God's involvement in your life with the next generation?

_____

_____

_____

_____

_____

_____

Why do you think God told Joel to tell his children and his children's children?

_____

_____

_____

_____

_____

_____

What are some organizational situations where unexpected chaos has arisen for you? How did you and your team handle these situations?

_____

_____

_____

_____

_____

In your own words, what is "intentional chaos"? Do you think intentional chaos is a necessary ingredient of a high-functioning team?

_____

_____

_____

_____

_____

What's your next big ministry idea? Take a moment to refine it by asking the following questions: What was? What is? What if? Even if?

_____

_____

_____

_____

_____

_____

_____

Does your church or organization have any stories of God's faithfulness or involvement in the past? Are you communicating them regularly and effectively?

_____

_____

_____

_____

_____

_____

_____

WHEN LEADERS LEAD

*"When leaders lead, God works,
and the world is changed."*

READING TIME

As you read Chapter 4: "When Leaders Lead" in *How Leaders Create Chaos*, reflect on the questions and scriptures.

REFLECT AND TAKE ACTION:

How can you take initiative in leading others while still following God and His plan? Do you feel that this is a difficult balance to achieve in your own life?

_____

_____

_____

_____

_____

Have you ever heard leadership be called "lonely"? How is this possible, since being a leader requires relationships with many different people?

_____

_____

_____

_____

_____

Do you believe that you currently lead with vision? Do those you lead understand where they are headed, and are they excited about the picture you're painting for them?

_____

_____

_____

_____

_____

> When Jesus came to the region of Caesarea Philippi, he asked his disciples, "Who do people say the Son of Man is?"
>
> They replied, "Some say John the Baptist; others say Elijah; and still others, Jeremiah or one of the prophets."
>
> "But what about you?" he asked. "Who do you say I am?"
>
> Matthew 16:13-15

Consider the scripture above and answer the following questions:

Why do you think the disciples had a hard time understanding and accepting what God was prompting Jesus to do?

_____

_____

_____

_____

_____

_____

If Jesus spent almost every day with the disciples once His ministry started, how much time should you spend with those you lead?

_____

_____

_____

_____

_____

_____

Of the leadership characteristics described in the "A Lion's Roar" section, which do you feel you best exhibit? Which do you feel you need to work on the most?

_____

_____

_____

_____

_____

_____

How do you and your organization respond to failure, generally speaking? What would be a better way to respond?

_____

_____

_____

_____

_____

_____

Do you think it's a good or bad idea to launch a new vision in the middle of a season of growth? Explain your answer.

_____

_____

_____

_____

_____

_____

_____

_____

Has God put a "perhaps" into your heart? If so, what is it?

_____

_____

_____

_____

_____

_____

_____

_____

ONE THING IS SURE

"When our expectations are unrealistic, we can't respond well to the hardships when they come."

READING TIME

As you read Chapter 5: "One Thing Is Sure" in *How Leaders Create Chaos*, reflect on the questions and scriptures.

REFLECT AND TAKE ACTION:

Do you expect adversity or obstacles to be in your path? Why or why not?

_____

_____

_____

_____

_____

_____

What do you think is the most important ingredient in preparing for hardships? How do you integrate this ingredient in your own leadership—or how do you need to do so?

_____

_____

_____

_____

_____

How can God use adversity to actually equip us for the road ahead?

_____

_____

_____

_____

_____

> *All these people were still living by faith when they died. They did not receive the things promised; they only saw them and welcomed them from a distance, admitting that they were foreigners and strangers on earth. People who say such things show that they are looking for a country of their own.*
>
> *Hebrews 11:13-14*

Consider the scripture above and answer the following questions:

Does the above verse encourage you or demotivate you? Explain your answer.

_____

_____

_____

_____

_____

_____

_____

What does the Bible mean when it calls these people foreigners and strangers?

_____

_____

_____

_____

_____

_____

_____

Why do you think it's important to recognize that these individuals did not get what they were promised in their earthly lifetimes?

_____

_____

_____

_____

_____

_____

Do you know anybody who is relentlessly (maybe even unrealistically) hopeful? How is your mindset affected when you're around this person?

_____

_____

_____

_____

_____

_____

Do you feel that you've mismanaged the expectations of those you lead in any ways? How can you reset those expectations so that they are more realistic?

_____

_____

_____

_____

_____

_____

Where do you want to bring the people you lead? What's holding you back from leading them there?

_____

_____

_____

_____

_____

_____

In a world of instant banking, five-minute microwave meals, and on-demand television, do you think it is harder than ever to be patient while a vision comes to fruition? Why or why not?

_____

_____

_____

_____

_____

_____

PASTORING THE PUSHBACK

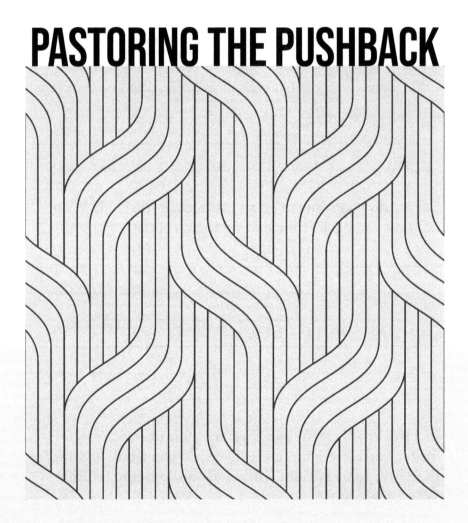

*"It's important for Pastors to expect pushback
and welcome it...
Anticipating hard questions gives us time
to prepare, to gather more information,
and to avoid reverse pushback."*

READING TIME

As you read Chapter 6: "Pastoring the Pushback" in *How Leaders Create Chaos*, reflect on the questions and scriptures.

REFLECT AND TAKE ACTION:

When have you encountered "push-back" in pastoral work or leadership? How did the situation make you feel, and what lessons did you learn from it?

_____

_____

_____

_____

_____

Do you think communication is impor-tant when pastoring the pushback? What other elements are necessary in order to do this well?

_____

_____

_____

_____

_____

Do you think all pushback is negative? How can pushback actually be benefi-cial to the team?

_____

_____

_____

_____

_____

> Jesus replied, "Very truly I tell you, no one can see the kingdom of God unless they are born again."
>
> "How can someone be born when they are old?" Nicodemus asked. "Surely they cannot enter a second time into their mother's womb to be born!"
>
> Jesus answered, "Very truly I tell you, no one can enter the kingdom of God unless they are born of water and the Spirit. Flesh gives birth to flesh, but the Spirit gives birth to spirit."
>
> John 3:3-6

Consider the scripture above and answer the following questions:

What is the real second birth that Christ is talking about to Nicodemus in this passage?

_____

_____

_____

_____

_____

_____

What can we learn from Jesus Christ's patient response to Nicodemus? How should we respond to pushback in our own leadership?

_____

_____

_____

_____

_____

_____

What does Jesus mean when He states, "the Spirit gives birth to spirit"?

_____

_____

_____

_____

_____

_____

When have you seen a leader receive pushback and handle it well? Describe the experience and what you learned from the situation.

_____

_____

_____

_____

_____

_____

How can pushback be handled wrongly? How have you seen this happen in your own journey?

_____

_____

_____

_____

_____

_____

Do you fear ambiguity? What purpose do you think ambiguity serves in your organization?

_____

_____

_____

_____

_____

_____

As the leader of the team, do you get those you lead? What can you do to put yourself into their shoes and better understand where they're coming from?

_____

_____

_____

_____

_____

_____

PREDICTABLE STAGES

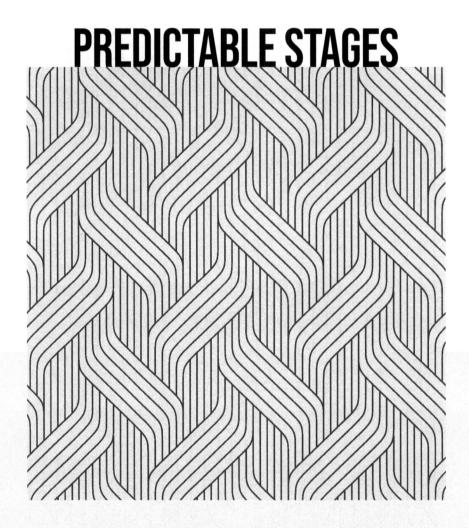

"Wise leaders have a powerful blend of humility (because they don't know the outcome of their decisions) and confidence (because God will have His way and teach important lessons no matter what happens)."

As you read
Chapter 7:
"Predictable
Stages" in
*How Leaders
Create Chaos*,
reflect on the
questions and
scriptures.

REFLECT AND TAKE ACTION:

Of the stages pictured in the diagram
in this chapter, which do you feel your
organization is in currently? What do
you think needs to happen to move you
to the next stage?

_____

_____

_____

_____

_____

_____

How can one lead with both humility
and confidence?

_____

_____

_____

_____

_____

_____

Do you think anticipation is an important ingredient when overcoming
hardship? Explain.

_____

_____

_____

_____

_____

_____

> We do not want you to be uninformed, brothers and sisters, about the troubles we experienced in the province of Asia. We were under great pressure, far beyond our ability to endure, so that we despaired of life itself. Indeed, we felt we had received the sentence of death. But this happened that we might not rely on ourselves but on God, who raises the dead.
>
> 2 Corinthians 1:8-9

Consider the scripture above and answer the following questions:

What does this verse reveal about sharing our hardships with others?

_____

_____

_____

_____

_____

_____

Do you think the Corinthians were motivated by the adversities that Paul overcame?

_____

_____

_____

_____

_____

_____

When have you been uplifted by the testimony of another Christian man, woman, or leader? Explain why their story was so helpful to you.

_____

_____

_____

_____

_____

_____

What processes should your organization start? What new programs, missions, or outreaches do you need to begin and why?

_____

_____

_____

_____

_____

_____

What does your organization need to stop? What process(es), program(s), or system(s) within your organization are no longer effective—maybe even slowing you down?

_____

_____

_____

_____

_____

_____

What should you sustain? What aspect(s) of your organization and its operations are working and providing a worthwhile return on investment?

_____

_____

_____

_____

_____

_____

What should your organization suspend? What processes are not effective, are losing your organization profit or influence, or need to be halted for the greater good of your vision?

_____

_____

_____

_____

_____

_____

What should your organization speed up? What is producing the best yields, and how can you take those things to the next level?

_____

_____

_____

_____

_____

_____

NOW AND LATER

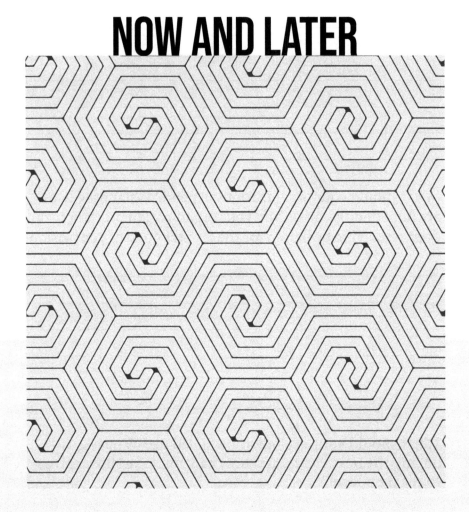

"Leaders need to wear bifocals, keeping an eye on the ultimate goal while shepherding the interactions of the team very closely."

As you read
Chapter 8:
"Now and
Later" in
*How Leaders
Create Chaos*,
reflect on the
questions and
scriptures.

REFLECT AND TAKE ACTION:

In what ways are you and your team unprepared for the looming chaos ahead?

_____

_____

_____

_____

_____

_____

What action steps can you start taking today in order to better prepare your people for inevitable chaos?

_____

_____

_____

_____

_____

_____

Of the nine leadership traits discussed in the "Do This, Do That" section, which do you feel you embody? How can those you lead see this trait in your leadership?

_____

_____

_____

_____

_____

> "Now then, just as the LORD promised, he has kept me alive for forty-five years since the time he said this to Moses, while Israel moved about in the wilderness. So here I am today, eighty-five years old! I am still as strong today as the day Moses sent me out; I'm just as vigorous to go out to battle now as I was then. Now give me this hill country that the LORD promised me that day...."
>
> Joshua 14:10-12

Consider the scripture above and answer the following questions:

Despite Joshua's age, he was still vigorous in his pursuit of the promise the Lord made to him. What can we learn from his vigor? Are you as vigorous and passionate as Joshua when pursuing the promises the Lord has made to you?

_____

_____

_____

_____

_____

_____

What "hill country" has God promised to you? What's stopping you from grasping it?

_____

_____

_____

_____

_____

_____

Do you ever find yourself struggling to continue to believe in God's promises? Why or why not?

_____

_____

_____

_____

_____

_____

Of the nine leadership traits discussed, which do you most need to work on? List them below, along with action steps that will move you closer to embodying those traits:

_____

_____

_____

_____

_____

_____

Has a promise from God ever taken longer to arrive than you anticipated? Has a promise ever arrived in a way you were not expecting? Describe the situation.

_____

_____

_____

_____

_____

_____

_____

_____

Of all the wisdom you learned throughout How Leaders Create Chaos, what will be your biggest takeaway, and how will you practically apply it to your leadership?

_____

_____

_____

_____

_____

_____

_____

_____

Lightning Source UK Ltd.
Milton Keynes UK
UKHW010651030123
414755UK00015B/659